MORE POLYTEKI

Celloduette im mittleren Schwierigkeitsgrad zum Erlernen musikalischer und technischer Fähigkeiten	Intermediate cello • technical accomplis

Polly Waterfield and Gillian Lubach

VORWORT • PREFACE

More Polytekniks enthält 12 neue Duette, die dazu angelegt sing, neue musikalische und technische Herausforderungen an fortgeschrittene Anfänger zu stellen. Die Stücke können entweder als Etüden oder einfach zum Spaß, um ihrer selbst willen, gespielt werden. Die untere Stimme ist in der Regel mehr für den Lehrer oder einen fortgeschritteneren Schüler bestimmt, obwohl einige der Duette auch für zwei Schüler gleichen Könnens geeignet sind, zum Beispiel *Schlaflied* und *Volkstümliche Rhapsodie*, in denen das Hauptabenteuer im Ensemblespiel besteht.

Wir hoffen, daß Lehrer in der Sammlung sowohl eine nützliche Ergänzung zu jedem Unterrichtsprogramm sehen als auch eine Quelle für ein anregendes und originelles Repertoire für fortgeschrittenere Spieler.

More Polytekniks contains 12 new duets designed to offer fresh musical and technical challenges for players of intermediate ability. The pieces may either be used as studies or as enjoyable music in their own right. The lower part is generally intended to be played by the teacher or a more advanced pupil, although some of the duets are suitable for two players of equal ability, for example *Lullaby* and *Folk Rhapsody*, where the main adventure is ensemble playing.

We hope that teachers will find the collection a valuable addition to any teaching programme, as well as a source of stimulating and original repertoire for developing players.

INHALT • CONTENTS

© 1994 by Faber Music Ltd
First published in 1994 by Faber Music Ltd
3 Queen Square London WC1N 3AU
Cover design by Lynette Williamson
German translations by Dorothee Göbel
Music processed by Wessex Music Services
Printed in England by Halstan & Co Ltd
All rights reserved

ISBN 0 571 51499 5

Lied und Tanz
Dritte Lage; Lagenwechsel

1

Song and Dance
Relaxed shifting to 3rd position

Schlaflied **2** Lullaby

Bitonalität; wechselnde Klangfarben *Bi-tonality, varying tone-colours*

PW

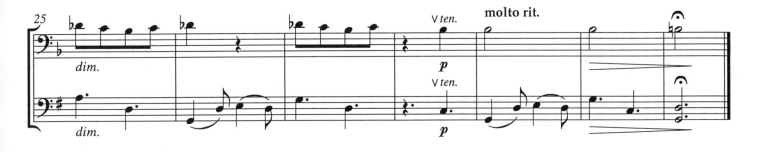

4

Kalamatianos

3

Kalamatianos

⅞-Takt; Bindungen über die Saite

⅞ time, slurred across-string bowings

With a gentle lilt

PW

Romanze **4** Romance

Reine und verminderte Septen   *Dominant and diminished 7ths*

Bulgarischer Tanz

Übermäßige Sekunden; Tenorschlüssel

5

Bulgarian Dance

Augmented 2nds/ Tenor Clef

'Bulgarian scale'

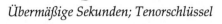

Ballade vom 'Bank Holiday'*

Akkorde, die 'con arco' bzw. 'pizzicato' gespielt werden

*=öffentlicher Feiertag

6

Bank Holiday Ballad

Bowed and pizzicato chords

GL

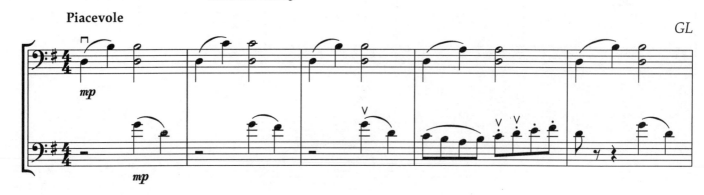

9

10

Atlantische Woge   **7**   Atlantic Swell
Flageolett-Töne   *Harmonics*

PW

Daumen nach oben!

Daumenlage; Tenorschlüssel

8

Thumbs Up!

Thumb position/Tenor clef

14

Nostalgie 9 Nostalgia

Zweite und dritte Lage; Bogeneinteilung; Synkopen   *2nd & 3rd positions, bow distribution, syncopation*

PW

15

* rit. and 🖙 2nd time only

Der Teufel in der Musik 10 The Devil in Music
Die verminderte Quinte *The diminished 5th*

Wheedling, not too slow

PW

faster and wild

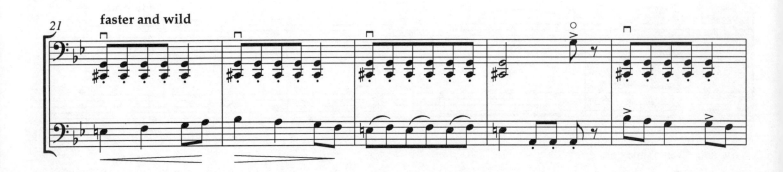

Volkstümliche Rhapsodie   **11**   Folk Rhapsody

Ensemble-Spiel; Wechsel von Tempo und Taktart; ad lib.-Spiel   *Ensemble playing, changes of tempo & metre, ad lib. playing*

Stately and with free expression

PW

Wellen 12 Making Waves

Vibrato; Tenorschlüssel *Vibrato, Tenor clef*

NOTES

1. *Song and Dance* . Here is a chance to appreciate the gentle mood of a melody played largely on the D string. The sound-quality should be matched when the music moves to the A string. In the *Allegretto* section the shifts from 1st to 2nd position are a preparation for bar 26.

2. *Lullaby* The upper part represents a screaming baby, and the lower part the mother trying to soothe it to sleep. Observe the contrasting dynamics, and control the bowing carefully in order to achieve different tone-colours by varying pressure, speed of bow and distance from the bridge.

3. *Kalamatianos* Rather than being counted in 7, this melody should be subdivided into 3:2:2. In the lower part a relaxed upper arm combined with steady and even bowing will produce the right sound.

4. *Romance* Dominant and diminished 7ths can be taught together, since they are closely related but very different in effect. The sound of the harmonies can then be emphasized: discordant and atmospheric for diminished; expansive and anticipatory for dominant. Ask pupils to spot them throughout the piece.

5. *Bulgarian Dance* This piece derives its exotic flavour from an unusual scale – a combination of major and harmonic minor. This scale (*given at the top of the piece) should be thoroughly assimilated before attempting the piece itself.

6. *Bank Holiday Ballad* Smooth and even bowing is needed for the 2- and 3-note chords and the upper notes of the 3-note ones should be held as long as possible. The 3- and 4-note pizzicato chords are played from bottom to top with the thumb angled slightly towards the bridge; while the 2-note ones are played with thumb and 2nd finger simultaneously. Pupils should aim for maximum resonance using vibrato where possible.

7. *Atlantic Swell* This piece exploits the atmospheric effect of harmonics. Pupils should be asked to find the notes which are actually sounding when the 3rd-position harmonics are played.

8. *Thumbs Up!* Before starting this piece, the pupil should play the following scale several times until the thumb position feels comfortable and the notes in the tenor clef are familiar:

At the Da Capo the hand should be very relaxed as it moves back into thumb position.

9. *Nostalgia* Organize the bowing in the first section so that there is enough for the long notes: very little should be used for the separate quavers. The trick with syncopations is to play smoothly through the tied-over first beats without making a bump.

10. *The Devil in Music* In the Middle Ages, the diminished 5th or tritone was known as the 'devil in music' owing to its discordant sound and destabilising harmonic effect. It was actually regarded as evil and prohibited by the Church! Listen carefully in order to play the piece well in tune.

11. *Folk Rhapsody* It should be fun for two friends to work out the ensemble, balance and tempo changes together. Or if a teacher/pupil duet is involved, the pupil should have a go at both parts, as they involve leading and folllowing in different places.

12. *Making Waves* Start with a large and rather slow vibrato, so that the complete movement (eight vibrations to the bar) may correspond to the quavers in the accompaniment. The open D in bar 4 can be 'warmed' by vibrating on the octave above.

ANMERKUNGEN

1. *Lied und Tanz* In diesem Stück kann man die zurückhaltende, zarte Wirkung einer Melodie hören, die primär auf der D-Saite gespielt wird. Diese besondere Klangqualität sollte auch nach dem Wechsel zur A-Saite erhalten bleiben. Im *Allegretto*-Teil dienen die Lagenwechsel von der ersten zur zweiten Lage der Vorbereitung auf Takt 26.

2. *Schlaflied* Die Oberstimme verkörpert hier das weinende Kind, während die Unterstimme die Mutter charakterisiert, die das Kind zum Schlafen zu bringen versucht. Man beachte die verschiedenen dynamischen Angaben und kontrolliere die Bogenführung sehr sorgfältig, um durch unterschiedlichen Bogendruck, Bogentempo und Abstand vom Steg verschiedene Klangfarben zu erreichen.

3. *Kalamatianos* Beim Erlernen dieser Melodie sollte man den Takt nicht in Zählzeiten von 1-7 einteilen, sondern stattdessen in Gruppen zu 3:2:2 unterteilen. In der unteren Stimme wird ein entspannter Oberarm in Verbindung mit ruhigem und gleichmäßigem Bogenstrich den richtigen Klang bewirken.

4. *Romanze* Reine und verminderte Septen können gleichzeitig erlernt werden, da sie eng miteinander verwandt, von ihrer Wirkung her gleichzeitig aber sehr verschieden sind. Der klangliche Wirkung der Harmonien kann dann noch betont werden: disharmonisch und schwebend für die verminderten, sich öffnend und vorwegnehmend für die reinen Septen. Der Schüler möge die verschiedenen Septen im Stück heraussuchen.

5. *Bulgarischer Tanz* Die ungewöhnliche Tonleiter, die diesem Stück zugrunde liegt, gibt ihm den exotischen Flair: eine Kombination von Dur und harmonischem Moll. Diese Skala – sie wird dem Stück vorangestellt – sollte man sich sorgfältig angeeignet haben, ehe man das Stück selber zu studieren beginnt.

6. *Ballade vom 'Bank Holiday'* Ein weicher und gleichmäßiger Strich ist die Voraussetzung für die hier zu spielenden Doppelgriffe und Dreiklänge; die oberen Töne der Dreiklänge sollten so lang wie möglich ausgehalten werden. Die *pizzicato* zu spielenden Drei- und Vierklänge werden von

unten nach oben gespielt, wobei der Daumen leicht zum Steg hin abgewinkelt ist. Die Doppelgriffe werden dagegen mit Daumen und zweitem Finger gleichzeitig gespielt. Die Schüler sollten sich um großes Klangvolumen bemühen und ein Vibrato wo immer möglich einsetzen.

7. *Atlantische Woge* Dieses Stück erforscht die klanglichen Effekte der Flageolett-Töne. Die Schüler sollten die Töne heraussuchen, die klingen, wenn in der dritten Lage Flageolett-Töne gespielt werden.

8. *Daumen nach oben!* Vor dem Erarbeiten dieses Stückes sollte der Schüler die folgende Tonleiter mehrmals spielen, bis er sich an die Daumenlage und den Tenorschlüssel gewöhnt hat.

Bei *Da Capo* sollte die Hand sehr entspannt sein, um leicht in die Daumenlage zurückzufinden.

9. *Nostalgie* Teilen Sie sich den Bogen im ersten Teil so ein, daß genug Bogen für die langen Noten vorhanden ist; für die einzelnen Viertel sollte nur wenig Bogen gebraucht werden. Die Synkopen lassen sich leicht spielen, wenn man bei den übergebundenen Taktzeiten weich weiterspielt, ohne diese zu betonen.

10. *Der Teufel in der Musik* Im Mittelalter galt die verminderte Quinte (auch 'Tritonus' genannt) wegen ihres dissonanten Klanges und ihrer alle harmonischen Prinzipien unterminierenden satztechnischen Wirkung als der 'Teufel in der Musik'. Die verminderte Quinte wurde als böse angesehen und von der Kirche verboten! Gut hinhören, um das Stück sauber zu spielen.

11. *Volkstümliche Rhapsodie* Es sollte zwei Freunden Spaß machen, in diesem Stück Zusammenspiel, Balance und Tempowechsel gemeinsam auszuarbeiten. Falls es sich um ein Duett Lehrer/Schüler handelt, sollte der Schüler beide Stimmen üben, da sie an verschiedenen Stellen jeweils führen oder begleiten.

12. *Wellen* Mit einem großen und recht langsamen Vibrato beginnen, so daß die gesamte Bewegung (acht Vibrationen pro Takt) mit den Achteln der Begleitung korrespondiert. In Takt 4 kann das 'd' der leeren Saite durch ein Vibrato eine Oktave höher etwas 'lebendiger' gestaltet werden.